Thoughts from Far and Near

Book II

with Best Wishes
Winifred Brown

Thoughts from Far and Near

Book II

Winifred Brown

The Pentland Press Limited
Edinburgh • Cambridge • Durham

© Winifred Brown 1994

First published in 1994 by
The Pentland Press Ltd.
1 Hutton Close
South Church
Bishop Auckland
Durham

All rights reserved.
Unauthorised duplication
contravenes existing laws.

ISBN 1 85821 xxx x

Typeset by CBS, Felixstowe, Suffolk
Printed and bound by Antony Rowe Ltd., Chippenham

To the Dad I never knew

Mr David Calvert

Contents

This is my Home

She stood and watched, in hooded coat,
Among her treasures true,
Her home, the pride of England fair,
Was burning, and she knew.

That though the walls would still be there,
The contents were all gone.
Her son was there to help and save,
The art-works, with the throng.

So many, many years have passed,
Since we left England's scene,
We crossed the ocean, knowing that
We still would have our Queen.

While living there, we watched her grow,
From babyhood to Queen,
Her childhood days with sister spent,
And on into the 'teen.

And then it was that true love came,
A union sure to please.
The time soon came, when duty called,
She took her place with ease.

She's having family troubles now,
We know she's not alone,
And now we try to think of how
She feels, 'This is my Home'.

Windsor Castle fire, Nov. 21st./92.

I Think of You

When the snow lay thick around,
Frost and ice upon the ground,
I think of you, dear, I think of you.

With winter's sun that hurts the eye,
With Northern Lights across the sky,
I think of you, dear, I think of you.

Now that the winter's here again
My skies are grey with winter rain,
You're not here, it's not the same.
I think of you.

Music in my Home

My home is filled with music
From very early morn,
The lilting tunes touch my ear,
By masters they are born.

Some bring back days of long ago
When we were far away,
And some are full of happy thoughts,
And tell of life today.

The marching bands that we recall,
The jig and waltzes too,
The haunting strains of violins
Keep memories ever new.

The organ and the oboe,
Piano and the flute,
Combine to make a pleasant sound
If senses are acute.

I'm thankful for the chance to hear
Recordings old and new,
Inventions we enjoy today,
We take for granted too.

The Old Chimney

There it stands, so cold and bare,
A sorry sight to see,
A memory of bygone days
And what it used to be.

It was a small but friendly house
A home just made for one,
A dear old lady and her pet,
And now the pet has gone.

For on that dreadful day in May
The flames devoured all,
The neighbours came, did what they could,
Before the walls did fall.

And now the only thing that's left
Is just the chimney bare,
Reminding her of cosy days
When she was living there.

All mixed up!

Sometimes things get all mixed up,
In families great or small,
The best laid plans that members make
Their dreamy castles fall.

All goes well until one day
Someone's interests change,
The truck that he no longer wants
Makes others rearrange.

The camper too will have to go
For 'tis a car he'll need,
His brother too will sell his truck,
There is no need to plead.

New plans they'll make, new goods they'll buy,
This time I hope 'twill please,
A more convenient mode of life,
They'll make the change with ease.

I hope that all will settle soon
And we can breathe again,
For when the branches twist and turn,
The tree must feel the strain.

Appreciation

In many different ways today
Our thoughts to others show,
For all the things they've done for us,
As on the way we go.

Advice they give when things go wrong,
A tasty morsel brought,
A book to read, some errands run,
A housing problem sought.

They've helped to get us where we are
In all our work and play,
And we must say our Thank-Yous
In some way to repay.

A country drive or flowers gay,
A cosy meal to share,
A book of chosen thoughts for her,
A present bought with care.

These are the things that we must do
If friends we hope to keep,
Appreciate a kindness shown
And happiness you'll reap.

The Big City

I went for a drive to the city today,
'Twas a long time since I was there,
We drove down the highway, the uphill and down,
We travelled with skill and with care.

The fields as we passed were all covered with snow,
The rocks from the mountainside fell,
The road with its cracks and its bumps and its holes,
Its own sorry story to tell.

The city was bustling and busy – but cold!
For winter time winds kept it so,
The streets were all clear, but the sky was so grey,
With clouds full of rain or of snow.

But soon, when the winter is all past and gone
And sunshine makes everything glow,
There'll be baskets of flowers on lamp standards hung,
And trees standing row upon row.

The park with its rosebeds and borders of flowers,
Forget-me-not, tulip and daff,
The ducks on the pond and seagulls there too,
The lawns kept trim by the staff.

The boats as they glide on the ocean so smooth,
The mountains we see far away,
This is the city we all love to see
As we travel just for the day.

The Old Wool Rug

As I cleaned my room today
I gazed upon the rug,
A little worn and woolly thing,
For toes it is so snug.

It's black with patterns woven in,
By tired hands it's true,
Reminding me of days gone by
Keeps memories ever new.

For it was made by native hands,
A payment made in trade,
Reminding me of happy days
When native friends we made.

Different Views

When my children gather round
Discussing points of view,
I marvel at their free debate,
On interests that are new.

They talk of golf and bowling too,
Of walks on mountain trail,
Of buying land, and property,
And boats that need no sail.

The varying ways of transport, too,
Some like a car so fine,
Others with a roving eye
Need one of strong design.

As I listen to their views,
Things that they dislike.
I think how boring it would be,
If we were all alike.

Encouragement

How often have we heard it said,
'I don't think that's for me!'
'I couldn't manage that I'm sure!'
'I couldn't pay the fee!'

But when another helps along,
The way seems all too clear,
The lessons learnt, the trials passed,
There's nothing more to fear.

A helping hand is all we need
When everything looks grey,
A kindly word – a friendly smile,
Will help us through the day.

Happy Days

I looked out of my window on my neighbour's garden fair,
And there her daughter, and her love were standing talking there.
It seems that only yesterday, they played with bat and ball,
When summer days were long and warm and even in the fall.

And now they visit Mother, dear, and sit 'neath shady tree,
A little one with bat and ball playing round their knee.
All too soon the happy years will go and memories stay,
But love remains, and family ties grow stronger every day.

Opening up the North

In the year of fifty-five
We travelled north to find
A livelihood for men and boys,
It brought peace of mind.

We found a city growing there
Just carved out of the bush,
Engines droning all the day,
At night – a welcome hush.

Birds that we'd not seen before,
Bears – and Oh! those flies!
The Northern Lights put on their show,
Such beauty in the skies.

The service held in classroom small,
Until the church was built,
Many nations worshipped there,
In sari and in kilt.

And down beside the water's edge
New homes and hospital,
The old stern wheeler moored there,
No need for Admiral!

The big ships loading at the quay,
They've brought the mineral ore,
They'll load the metal, moulded true,
And sail for distant shore.

The village nestling by the sea,
Our native brothers there,
The trading post like days of yore,
With products all can share.

The city grew, the smelter too,
And now we're far away,
Some day we'll visit all our friends
Upon a holiday.

Together again

I'm glad that you could come today,
I've missed your friendly smile,
So now you're here, we have a chance,
To talk – just for a while.

The picnic on the sandy beach,
And in the garden fair,
The holiday on a foreign shore,
It was a grand affair.

You roamed the heather on the moor,
You basked in the island sun,
You met the old folks, young ones, too,
Your day was never done.

There's some who visit far and wide,
They find new paths to roam,
But others cannot get away,
So they just stay at home.

But here we are together now,
Faithful friends so true,
Refreshed, with hope and courage, too,
To face the tasks anew.

The Garden Party

My garden looks gay, on days like today,
The green, and the flower bouquet,
The coloured umbrellas, and tables laid,
The stream, and the ferns in the glade.

My garden sounds gay, on days like today,
The laughter, the voices, the play,
The joy that we know, as our friendship we show,
Makes everyone's heart all a-glow.

My garden is gay, in the eve of today,
For memories linger alway,
The birds in the trees, and the soft evening breeze,
I'm grateful for days like these.

Beginning again

In the twilight of our years,
There always comes a time,
A time when we begin again,
The hill that we must climb.

We've had our ups and downs, my dear,
The laughter and the tears,
The loved ones who have gone before,
Have left us full of fears.

We feel the need for rest and care,
A haven to enjoy,
A fellowship of fellowman,
That nothing can destroy.

Our needs are few, and simple, too,
There's not much we desire,
A cosy room, a book to read,
A chair beside the fire.

A window taking in the view,
The lawn, the lake, a tree,
A simple meal, a bed to rest,
A friend, a cup of tea.

O, help us to begin again,
Dear Lord, stay by our side,
Help us find contentment there,
In our Eventide.

My Workshop

I love my little workshop,
My kitchen, neat and trim,
With canisters of red and white,
And yellow round the rim.

The counters and the cupboards,
My tools all safe within,
My cups and saucers, knives and forks,
And my old rolling pin.

The products of my workshop,
The best that I can bake,
Nothing fancy – wholesome, plain,
Is all that I can make.

I hope that I can please them,
As supper I prepare,
For when the evening shadows fall,
My reward is there.

My Garden

My garden is a lovely place at any time of year,
But mostly when the roses are a-blooming everywhere,
There's climbers, and the hybrid teas, and floribundas too,
And there upon the hedge I see a wild one peeping through.

The lilac trees that bring such joy when May comes round again,
Their fragrance is a pleasure sweet, in sunshine or in rain,
Reminding us of vows we made when we were twenty-one,
So long ago and far away, our parents now are gone.

In spring the tulips and the daffs, the snowdrops, crocus, too,
The hyacinth, the bluebell, and the primrose are now due,
The apple, pear and cherry blossoms, make a pretty show,
Oh, is there a more lovely sight, if so I'd like to know.

In a bed set in the lawn, geraniums there,
With blue and white along the edge,
They're planted with such care,
The pansies, with their faces lifted up to the Sun,
The laurels and the climbing vines, whose life is never done.

After the rain, there's the song of the bird, the stirring hum of a bee,
There's no such place in all the world, brings so much peace to me,
The dew on a rose, in the morning sun glows,
The flutter of wings in the air,
These are the marvels, they're just Heaven sent,
They're signs just to tell me He's there.

The Little Kirk

There's a dear little church on the brow of the hill,
A place where there's comfort and rest,
It's somewhere to go, if afraid or upset,
A haven – the house of the blest.

Its built, oh so strong, with the walls made of logs,
And a spire pointing up to the sky,
A set of stone steps with a railing so firm,
And a light there, when evening is nigh.

The pews, all hand-made, with their little brass plaques,
The organ adds tone to the scene,
The rest of the furnishing, all of the same,
The flooring is always so clean.

Oh for rest and quiet thought,
Time to be silent and still,
Help me to find my peace of mind,
In the church on the brow of the hill.

My Blessings

As I sit when evening falls,
Thinking of the day,
And all the problems that it brought,
And many that will stay.

I think of all the good things,
That come to me each day,
The health of all my family,
Their love and care alway.

The nearness of my dearest one,
His love so rich and rare,
The children, and the friends we have,
There's nothing to compare.

The smiles, the laughter and the songs,
The home where we may rest,
The little pleasures we enjoy,
Our lives are truly blest.

To a Robin

See him out there, out there on the lawn,
Hear him in the tree,
The singing messenger of Spring,
Brings hope for you and me.

New hopes for Spring and Summer skies,
Forget the winter long,
With wind and rain, and snow and ice,
Just listen to his song.

He sings of nests of woven grass,
Of sticks and straw and clay,
Of tiny eggs, so warm and snug,
Awaiting their great day.

Entranced, we hear the wild bird sing,
Oh, herald of the Spring!
Singing in the garden there,
'Ere soon he takes to wing.

Dreams of Home

I had a dream the other day,
'Twas not while in my bed,
I've had this daydream many times,
And many tears were shed.

I was nine thousand miles away,
Across the ocean wide,
How I wish my dream would be
More real in its stride.

A half an acre, that was all,
But it was all my land,
A piece of this dear blessed realm,
On which my feet can stand.

The countryside with hills and dales,
And English oaks abound,
With flowering shrubs, and plants, and lawns,
A rockery too I found.

The greenhouse needs a touch of paint,
A little, here and there,
I'll plant my seedlings in the soil,
And nurture them with care.

In Spring, 'twill be a sight to see,
For now it is the Fall,
The snowdrops, then the crocus, too,
And daffodils, so tall.

The tulips, and the hyacinth,
And lots of bluebells, too,
All underneath the chestnut tree,
A cloud of misty blue.

I had a table for the birds,
Blue tits, my robins too,
A chaffinch, and a blackbird sang,
Just as they used to do.

I had the mailman at my door,
Bringing all my mail,
The post box, still set in the wall,
Down by the village rail.

My house was heated perfectly,
Just as a good house should,
The garage, well! I'll have to fix,
The car objects, it should!!

When I think of days gone by,
How true these dreams are bred,
Memories of scenes I've stored,
Away inside my head.

When I hear from one at 'home',
Who knows just what to say,
My photogenic mind can see,
What he means to portray!!

The Little Gift Shop

There's a little shop I know,
With gifts of every kind,
For those who lie on beds of pain,
There's something they can find.

There's little things for people small,
So very small and new,
A card, a book, a flower sweet,
A gift with love so true .

A little cart is pushed around,
Into every ward,
For those who cannot find their way,
For them, a rich reward.

And those that care for all the gifts,
Be they large or small,
Their time and love are freely given,
A benefit to all.

Good Luck and God Bless

As children all have grown,
From babes to manhood now,
On this graduation day,
My youngest takes his bow.

In this torn and troubled world,
With talk of war and stress,
I pray my love will guide him through,
Good Luck and may God Bless!

Howard

My Lilies

Whenever I travel the highway broad,
Going north, around the bend,
I stop and I stare at the waterfall there,
A spot where hearts can mend.

And there I see, when spring is here,
My lilies, slender, fair,
Swaying in the wind and spray,
How did they get up there?

A little seed takes many years,
To make this pretty sight,
A miracle of nature, clinging
On the rocks so tight.

And then one day as I passed by,
My heart was filled with gloom,
My lilies were no longer seen,
Had someone sealed their doom?

But, no, for later in the spring,
I travelled there to see,
My lilies, waving, calling me,
I clapped my hands with glee.

Oh may these joys of nature stay,
To gladden every heart,
To help us see that someone cares,
And how He plays his part.

She Went Away

She went away, one day in May,
She had to go alone,
She had a meeting with her Lord,
The journey was her own.

But we shall meet again some day,
In that distant land,
She's happy there, with friends who share,
Their glory, hand in hand.

Patience

He sits up there on the top of the pole,
The white bird from the sea,
He circles around then back to his perch,
Waiting so patiently.

He knows my neighbour will soon appear,
His feathered friends to feed,
Then down he'll fly, the table's spread,
With tasty bits they need.

Breakfast over, off he goes,
Calling as he flies,
What a joy to see the birds,
From morn till daylight dies.

Evening Magic

Have you been down to the bay,
To see the freighters there?
You must go down when night is nigh,
There's magic in the air.

The night I went, I counted ten,
All grouped around the bay,
The mountains, in the setting sun,
At the close of day.

And as I watched in gathering gloom,
Each ship, a blaze of light,
Shone out across the waters calm,
A picture in the night.

The coloured lights a pathway made,
Together with the moon,
I'm glad I had the chance to see,
For they'll be gone so soon.

Precious Gifts

'All good gifts around us
Are sent from heaven above',
The old, old lines we know so well,
That speak to us of Love.

Once a year this busy world,
Just pauses for a spell,
Remembering God's gift to man,
The child, Emmanuel.

The wonder and the glory of
The Christmastide we see,
The magic and the beauty of
A child's first Christmas tree.

Help us, Lord, amid the strife
Of this our war-torn earth,
To give the gift of inward peace
And Faith, and Love and Mirth.

Look Upward

When all is well, and hopes are high,
There's sunny days ahead,
So much to see, so much to do,
I'll spin a stronger thread.

I'll weave a life of Faith and Love,
With one aim to pursue,
Let me not waste my time today,
My purpose is in view.

And if I fall along the way,
I hope that I may bear,
The pain and trials that ensue,
And sink not in despair.

For Life is but a mountain road,
Look upward and you'll see,
The sunlight gleaming round the bend,
Towards eternity.

Sounds of Living

I've just been in my garden fair,
Hanging out the clothes,
I heard the sounds of living,
As I hung out these and those.

The lawnmower just across the fence,
The little car next door,
The children as they laugh and play,
They're only three and four.

I heard the trucks with timber cut,
And those that carry logs,
The milk and bread vans passing by,
The barking of the dogs.

I heard the clicking of the keys,
The sign the mail arrives,
I wonder if there's mail from home,
To tell of other lives.

I'm glad that I can hear the sounds,
Of living day by day,
It's then I know I'm not alone,
Upon the Life's highway.

My Cactus Flower

I have some cacti in my home,
Of many varying kinds,
To some they may not look so good,
Just those with different minds.

From Easter on, for many months,
Their blossoms I enjoy,
But one, a prickly funny thing,
Has never brought me joy.

But oh, what's this? a fluffy shoot,
It grew and grew and grew,

And then one night it opened wide,
I gazed at something new.

It was a most exquisite bloom,
The like I've never seen,
A white and wondrous blossom rare,
Tis gone! Has't ever been?

The plant looks just the same to me,
But I can still recall,
When once in twenty years I saw,
A sight that captured all.

I'm Home Again

I'm home again! Oh, blessed day!
The boys and dear old dad,
The garden, – goodness how it's grown!
The good rows and the bad.

The lawns so green and newly cut,
The roses in full bloom,
Our cat, the little fluffy pet,
Follows, room to room.

The whistle as the train goes by,
The laughter in the yard,
As men work on their trucks and things,
The work is fun, though hard.

For weeks I've laid on beds of pain,
At home and far away,
So many people feeling thus,
So many worse, they say.

But oh! the friends, the cards, the flowers,
Thank you, one and all!
And for the prayers I know were said,
They brought me through it all.

The Way to go

The Lord is my Shepherd, we hear them say,
I know I'll not want this day,
For down in green pastures with friends fond and true,
The waters are still so blue.

He helps and He guides me, my soul in His care,
He leads me along, I'm aware,
He keeps me each day in the Christian way,
For sisters and brothers, I pray.

I pray as they walk through the Valley of Death,
That He will be there with each breath,
To help and encourage when all else seems lost,
And never once counting the cost.

He feeds and clothes me in these troubled times,
With wars in the furthermost climes,
His love for me touches my heart and my hand,
My brother, will you take the stand?

Surely your goodness will follow along,
The days of my life like a song,
For if I can help someone back to the fold,
My life will be richer, I'm told.

So, take heart my sisters and brothers, too,
Take courage and start life anew,
And if by your actions a life you can save,
You may dwell in the house that He gave.

Just Carrying On

When our friends have gone ahead,
We feel the loss so deep,
But we must not be in despair,
For they are but asleep.

Asleep until God's lamp of love,
Awakes them to the light,
Dear Guardian Angel, walk with me,
Until my soul takes flight.

Until that day we must be strong,
And do the work at hand,
We'll take it up and carry on,
Where once they took the stand.

How weary we should grow of it,
Were sunshine all the way,
There would be no rainbows,
If the skies were never grey.

So, my friends, we'll journey on,
The pleasures and the pains,
Disappointment and success,
The losses and the gains.

We must not look for easy paths,
The road is hard to climb,
For this is life, you've got to keep,
On trying all the time.

He's Leaving

What am I thinking of today,
For this is New Years Day?
A day of beginning something new,
Something good to say.

But here I am, I'm all mixed up,
And the reason why,
Because my boy is leaving home,
A new life for to try.

He won't be going far away,
He's moving into town,
I know he'll come and see me soon,
I shouldn't really frown.

But there are thoughts that I must keep,
Locked inside my heart,
Until the day I hear him say,
'Until death do us part'.

They're Going Away

What are my thoughts on this fine Spring day?
They're going – they're going away,
They took their vows just yesterday,
And now they're going away.

The world seems smaller, year by year,
I should not shed a tear,
For though there may be miles between,
The mail will oft' be seen.

I ask, for them, much happiness,
A world that's free of stress,
And for a bright tomorrow,
As on their way they go.

But as for me, I will agree,
The empty chairs, I see,
I'm sure I'll shed a tear today,
They're going, they're going away.

Sleep

'Ere I lay me down to sleep,
Pray the Lord my soul to keep,
As a child, and years between,
Thoughts like these my prayers would mean.

My busy days are filled with toil
From things abusive I recoil,
When the moon is in the sky,
Happy in my bed I lie.

Days of worry, days of glee,
These are not unknown to me,
But at night I need the rest,
Hours of sleep with which I'm blest.

Sometimes dreams disturb the night,
When the day had not gone right,
But they pass, and with the dawn,
I am strengthened for the morn.

How I need these hours of sleep,
Never need to count my sheep,
Refreshed when morning light appears,
To help along the passing years.

Joy at Easter

Easter is a time of joy,
With new life all around,
A time for us to start again,
To build the life we've found.

And Oh! the joy that we have felt,
Upon this Easter Day,
When one that we had thought was lost,
Was found along the way.

The baby that was born that day,
So many years ago,
My son so proud, so full of love,
The mother all aglow.

And now the child is all grown-up,
With baby of her own,
My son has found her, happy day!
My, how the years have flown!

He brought her here at Eastertide,
A happy time for all,
With, brothers, sisters, friends to share,
The memories we recall.

Though there may be miles between,
I know we'll always share,
This happy Eastertide we showed,
How very much we care.

For now our family tree has grown,
Branches, tender new,
And Dad and I must keep them all,
Together, strong and true.

Ian and Debbie

Great-Grands

My son came to my home today,
His visit was a treat,
He travels so much on these days,
We seldom ever meet.

He gave me a photograph,
Three little children there,
His daughter's little ones, so cute,
My little great-grands there.

I hope one day to meet them all,
They live so far away,
But he can see them, and I know,
I'll see them some fine day.

Debbie

Beyond the Moon

When the moon is shining bright,
And all the world is still,
Remember how we used to watch,
Just beyond the hill.

We'd stand together, hand in hand,
And watch the clouds go by,
We'd think of nights like this we've seen,
My! how the years do fly.

So, when the moon is shining bright,
And all the world is still,
Remember I'll be waiting there,
Just beyond the hill.

Memories of Britain

I've just been sitting in my garden,
Watching all the world go by,
Thinking of the past few weeks,
When we three had to fly.

To fly to Britain miles away,
Across the ocean wide,
With many friends both young and old,
Companions side by side.

We travelled o'er that pleasant land,
Two thousand miles and more,
We saw the abbeys, churches, too,
And boats along the shore.

We took a steamer on the lake,
It was a pleasant sail,
The swans, and later, peacocks too,
Showing off their tail.

We saw so many lambs and sheep,
And fields with walls of stone,
We walked the paths the Romans trod,
And we were not alone.

For thirty-nine plus two, there were,
Who travelled mile on mile,
The roads so narrow where we went,
It brought us many a smile.

'Breathe in!' the escort told us,
As cars we had to pass,
The driver with his expert eye,
Drove safely o'er the pass.

We saw the ponies on the moors,
We ate our Devonshire cream,
The little train of narrow gauge,
The engine puffing steam.

We made a stop along the way,
A photo for to take,
Of all the thirty-nine plus two,
A memory for to make.

We made a wedding in pretence,
Beside the anvil there,
The bridal couple, parents too,
For all of us to share.

The laughter and the merriment,
Continued all the way,
And so the time went gaily by,
Until the goodbye day.

1989

Happy Birthday, Dear

I know a man, a quiet man,
We've lived here, side by side,
For fifty years and more beside,
Our dreams were sorely tried.

I give him all the love I can,
As much as I can spare,
But there are five more, just like him,
And they must have their share.

May we be spared, a few years more,
To see their dreams come true,
And now I wish this gentle man,
Birthday wishes, too.

Golden Years

Another year has come and gone,
The golden ones are here,
But here we are together, dear,
Dreaming without fear.

We've made the journey, side by side,
The road was often rough,
We've had our ups and downs, my love,
Sometimes the work was tough.

But you were made for me, my love,
We travelled hand in hand,
God knew our love would stand the test,
We met each new demand.

And as the boys all grew, my love,
They married, nearly all,
And now their children gather round,
With golden wedding call.

And now, my dear, we know not what,
May come in years ahead,
We only know our love is strong,
Just as the day we wed.

23rd May 1986

The Meaning of Christmas

Oh Lord, we think of years gone by,
A baby boy was born,
He brought with him new life for all,
Upon that Christmas morn.

They say His name was Jesus,
They thought Him Joseph's son,
But God above, who taught Him love,
And how a soul is won.

And now, O Lord, we gather round,
We sing, ' O! Silent Night',
And hope that through the year the world,
Will come to see the Light.

She's Twenty-one Today

And here we are, the years have flown,
She's twenty-one today.
She graduated, passed the test,
And now she's on her own.

Her Mother smiling, ever there,
Has trained her in her trade,
'Twas what she wanted, all these years,
And now her future's made.

And now she's left this town of ours,
The city called her there,
She found her job, she found her beau,
And everything looked fair.

For now she's in the business world,
With progress all around,
There'll be changes now and then,
Till her own place be found.

And now, my grandchild, go your way,
With health, and peace, alway,
You're in my prayers, the family, too,
And may God guide your way.

Lorelei

Hands Across the Sea

There is a man, a quiet man,
A native of our land,
His parents came, long years ago,
To join our growing band.

They had their ups and downs, we know,
Their lives were hard to bear,
They'd left their home, across the seas,
And all of those who care.

But families grow, and theirs did too,
They scattered, far and wide,
But some there were who stayed at home,
Their garden would provide.

But this dear man, his garden found,
His loved one by his side,
A son and heir, to share their joy,
Fulfilled his family pride.

And now he shares his garden world,
With others who will care,
With him, his loved one, and his son,
They'll keep the city fair.

Hito

For the Love of a Garden

When I was young and in my teens,
I worked with English soil,
My friend and I and others, too,
Enjoyed our daily toil.

As Autumn days came round again,
'Twas time to think of Spring,
We planted bulbs of every sort,
To bloom when Church bells ring.

For Eastertime was busy there,
The boxes to be made,
To fill the orders from afar,
I packed them, every shade.

Then came the time when men would work,
To sow the salad greens,
And all the plants, in house of glass,
For summertime, t'would seem.

And now my son, my youngest son,
Is working with the soil,
A different country, different folks,
And how he loves his toil.

He views the landscape, great or small,
And studies all his plan,
His life-long partner by his side,
To help him all she can.

And there is one, who's always there,
His loved one by his side,
Together they will build a dream,
And there they'll all abide.

Howard

The Tower of Strength

Long years ago, and far away,
Way back in forty-nine,
My Mother joined the heavenly host,
The ones we call divine.

There was my husband, children four,
That helped to keep me strong,
But there was one, though only nine,
Who helped us all along.

He took her place, from that day on,
When half my life was spent,
He did the things that she would do,
He seemed to be content.

And as the years rolled on apace,
We travelled far and wide,
His nature, helping young and old,
He took it in his stride.

And now my birthday's here again,
Both he and I need care,
He hides his own pain, as before,
For others need his care.

Roland

How Long, Lord?

As the years go drifting by,
I often wonder why,
Why so many, some so young,
Are called away to die.

I've seen so many changes made,
Since I saw the light of day,
From cobblestones, to highway wide,
To help us on our way.

The horse and buggy days are gone,
For speed is now in line,
What do we do with the time we save?
How do we spend the time?

I've gone through wireless, radio, too,
To satellites and space,
And all the gadgets in between,
To help us with this race.

There are so many things today,
That I find hard to do,
But I must use up all my time,
There's much that I can do.

I have learned to be content,
However hard the climb,
For I must fill each moment, Lord,
You only, know the time!

What is a Friend?

Someone rang my bell today,
A friend so staunch and true,
She came to see just how I was,
And brought a job to do.

For I can sit here in my chair,
And do this simple task,
To help the ones who need our care,
It's not that much to ask.

She stayed a while, with cup in hand,
We talked of many things,
She does not know how much it means,
And how much joy it brings.

To have a friend to ring my bell,
And tell me all the news,
To stay awhile, and laugh awhile,
Exchange each other's views.

Oh may there always be a friend,
To give me jobs to do,
To keep me helping all I can,
To help the whole day through.

Do You Remember Me?

I met a man, a quiet man,
While I was out today,
He said 'Good morning', I did too,
He smiled, each went our way.

I wonder if he really knows,
How many years have flown?
Since first he knew me, children too,
My how they all have grown!

It must be thirty years ago,
When we were in our prime,
And now I see him, once a week,
I watch him every time.

For he has had his troubles too,
He's well aware of pain,
Now he's proud to help his son,
He walks without his cane.

And now I wish, for this dear man,
And all his family, too,
A future filled with happiness,
With love and good health, too.

Once a Week!

I met a friend, a thoughtful friend,
Don't even know her name,
We meet each other once a week,
The purpose is the same.

We sit there, just an hour or so,
While nimble fingers fly,
Making us feel – Oh, so good!
My! How the weeks go by!

I hope for her, good wishes true,
I hope to see her soon,
For sometimes, that one hour a week,
Is my big treat, my own!

Why – Lord – Why?

My son took me to church today.
He takes me when he can,
I did not know, before I went,
But as the day began.

I noticed how much pain he had,
He could not hide it all,
I wanted him to take me home,
But no – he would stand tall.

He stood and sang the carols old,
Supported by the pew,
He read the Good Book line by line,
The words he also knew.

He took the bread, he took the juice,
For he'll not touch the wine,
For many years he's been in pain,
While waiting for some sign.

That someone, somewhere in this world,
Has knowledge, he would try,
Restore his faith in life today,
I ask, Oh, Why – Lord – Why?

Roland

Oh Happy Day!

Oh! happy day, this Christmas Day!
My grandson's home again!
He had to try the world outside,
The sunshine and the rain.

He had to learn the right from wrong,
The straight and narrow way,
He saw the light, and left the friend,
Who made him go astray.

He found a friend, Oh! such a friend,
Her life was what he sought,
They found together something good,
Something that can't be bought.

She taught him that there is a way,
A cleaner life for him,
She showed him how to love and care,
For those whose days seem grim.

I hope for them a future bright,
When studies are all through,
For they had found, their parents see,
A love, that's staunch and true.

The End of an Era

At Christmas Time in ninety-one,
There were some changes made,
The little tree, which every year,
We trimmed it, with some aid.

My youngest son had bought the tree,
Just twenty-five years past,
He trimmed it for me, when he could,
But this year was the last.

I had some holly, cards as well,
And plants for all to see,
My crib, my centrepiece was there,
As always it shall be.

My Christmas letter, I have sent
For thirty-six years past,
Since first I came to this fair land,
Is one more custom past.

My children now have left the nest,
With families of their own,
And now my dear one, and our son,
Live quietly on our own.

I wish for you a Christmas-time,
With happiness and joy,
A year to follow, good health, too,
That you may all enjoy.

1992

57

I'll Always Remember You!

Birthdays, anniversaries, too,
And Christmas Season, yes,
All these special days each year,
Come round for God to bless.

But as the years go swiftly past,
And families still grow,
For those of us on income fixed,
Don't know which way to go!

We love you all so very much,
And always will remember,
Your special days as they come round,
From January to December.

So, please accept our wishes true,
And keep them in your heart,
A greeting card, with words to suit,
And blessings to impart!

1991

58

The Young Ones

I saw, while I was out today,
A sight that warmed me through,
A couple, starting out in life,
I suppose that's nothing new.

But these two – they're a special pair
The girl, the daughter fair,
Of one, that I hold dear to me,
She treats me with such care.

But as she sat there in her chair,
Her puppy on her knee,
I wished that I possessed the skill,
To paint what I could see.

For what I saw, the bloom of youth,
There was such beauty there,
Her Mother, with such expert hands,
Her loved one in her care.

And Mother smoothed and groomed his hair,
The style I like to see,
I think I saw the loving care,
With which she touched his hair.

And now, I wish, for these dear folks,
A future, full of hope,
Of dreams, and schemes, and all those things,
With which they'll have to cope!

Betrayed

When you work your best each day,
In spite of crippling pain,
You work long after time each day,
Ensure no jobs remain.

You love the work, you've made your plans,
To stay and give your best,
For all the time that's left to you,
And may the time be blest.

They've told you many times before,
Your presence there they need,
Your knowledge seems the thing they want,
There is no need to plead.

So why, just when the sick bed calls,
They cast you on one side?
Your future seems uncertain now,
You'll keep the hurt inside.

THIS BOOK WAS DEDICATED TO MY
FATHER.--MR. DAVID CALVERT. J.P.
================================
for his distinguished personality, and
career, as noted by these gentlemen.
================================

Quoted by:- the Rev. Charles Humble.
-------------- --------------------------------

      "David Calvert, was a favourite with all of us here at the Church.
As Ministers, he had an unqualified appreciation and affection. I never
knew him to be fitful, or variable, in his relations with his fellow-
workers. I remember, so well, his quiet, thoughtful, but intense and
fervent prayers, on a Sunday evening. He was a kindly, wise, and strong
minded man. His personality imparted, tone and character, to the
composite life of the Church."--

================================

     "HE BEING DEAD YET SPEAKETH"!--
================================

Quoted by:- the Rev. E.B. Storr.
----------- ------------------------

      "The Howden-le-Wear, Church, was strong and steady-going.
David Calvert, was the most prominent figure. He was the choir-master,
and many offices, I can't remember, but he was by social position, gift,
character, and experience, the natural leader of the Church."--

================================

Quoted by:- the Rev. J.W. Collinwood.
----------- -----------------------------------

      "David Calvert, was a man of quite exceptional ability and
Character, - wise in judgment, - sane, in counsel - and utterly devoted to
the Church. His passing, in September, 1915, was a great loss,
especially, to his own Church in Howden-le-Wear."--

================================

     AT THE TIME HE DIED IN 1915, I was only TEN MONTHS
old..which accounts for the heading on this book.

                       Winnifred Brown
                       ============

The Lost Ticket

When I was young, and just a child,
Way back in twenty-six,
I travelled on the train each day,
'Twas the eight thirty-six.

We met together, rushing round,
With contracts in our hands,
A most important 'passport' that,
We showed upon demand.

And then one day, I lost my pass,
Nowhere could it be found,
And at that time our life was hard,
We counted every pound.

Although I was so very young,
I knew my Lord was near,
I knew that prayers were answered, too,
In ways some thought were queer.

When walking home one autumn day,
I asked Him for some sign,
When suddenly, I had a thought,
'Twas in this coat of mine!

My coat was brown, with fur for trim,
But, alas, it had no pocket,
And Mother made one, just inside,
To hold my precious docket!

And as I felt the hem below,
Oh! joy beyond compare!
There it was, all safe and sound,
The pocket needs repair.

Little things like this we hold
Within our memory store,
A meeting with an old, old, friend,
Reminds us of these and more.

A True Volunteer

There is a man, a quiet man,
He loves the great outdoors,
He's not a man for city life
With all its concrete floors.

Give him a floor of moss and grass,
Rocks and fallen trees,
Beaver, birds, and eagles, too.
All wanting to be free.

He's always there, no matter when,
For searches near or far,
He'll mend a roof, he'll dig a ditch,
No matter where they are.

He works among the old, old things,
The relics of the past,
He helps restore them, making sure,
For years to come, they'll last.

He tends the many parks and trails,
His first love since he came,
His faithful friends have rallied round,
Just to bless his name.

Roland 1992

Golden Days

So here we are, the Golden Days,
The way's been hard and long,
We left our Homeland, years ago,
Were we right or wrong?

Our boys have grown, and left the nest,
They married, one and all,
And now their children gather round,
The small ones, and the tall.

We've had our troubled times, my dear,
We travelled hand in hand,
God knew our love would stand the test,
We met each new demand.

And now, my dear, we know not what
May lie in years ahead,
We only know our love is strong,
Just as the day we wed.

Charles and Rosina

There is no Greater Love

His life is more than half way past,
He lives it well and true,
To all who know him, work or play,
Each day is filled anew.

He loves his boys, some far away,
And all his family, too,
But most of all, he'll share his life,
With one, till life is through.

She needs his care, in many ways,
But what is that to him?
They have so many memories stored,
Some good ones, some are grim.

They live their lives, just day by day,
Example to us all,
There is so much that they can do,
Problems, great or small.

They know not what may lie ahead,
But happy they will be,
I only hope that home to them,
Is where their hearts will be.

My Graduation Girl

I just can't find the words I want,
To say to you today,
The years of study are all through,
And now you're on your way.

On your way to something new,
New people, places, life,
You'll find the world a cold hard place,
Where evil things are rife.

But you will know just what to do,
You've learnt your lessons well,
Your parents, too, have shown they care,
In training you so well.

But it is your nature, dear,
That I like most of all,
You were there when needed most,
In Springtime and in Fall.

And now, my dear, keep strong and true,
I hope you find your dreams,
A dream that only two can share,
Good Luck, God Bless your schemes.

Jody 1992

The Extra Mile

What do you say, when your heart is full
And 'Thank-you' isn't enough?
They gave their time and labour, too,
Sometimes the work was rough.

They work each day among the things,
The green and living things,
That God intended they should do,
What happiness it brings!

To those of us, the older ones,
Who love their garden fair,
It means so much to folks like us,
To have someone to care.

But these dear folks, from far away,
They knew there was a need,
And so they did what should be done,
There was no need to plead.

They helped to make what time is left,
A happier place for all,
Who live here, in this garden fair,
In Springtime and in Fall.

Howard and Freda

You're Always There

You're always there, when needed most,
No matter where or when,
But this time was a special time,
There were some nine or ten.

They came from near or far away,
And you two did your part,
You planned, and schemed, as you can do,
Each one of you took part.

You brought something to two old folks,
A need they both required,
They struggled quietly, year by year,
Until they got too tired.

And so you all stepped in to help,
To make our life a dream,
The garden, which is Dad's domain,
Made easier with your scheme.

Stuart and Carol

A Friend in Need

I met a friend at home today,
She comes from overseas,
Like me, she made this country home,
Her life it seems to please.

She did her lessons, year by year,
And now she has her trade,
Where she devotes what time she has,
To help those needing aid.

She asked her questions, one by one,
She knows her work so well,
I hope she knows how much it meant,
To all who herein dwell.

She took my hand, so old yet soft,
And chatted for a while,
My dear one, showed her all around,
His garden made her smile.

This country is a home to us,
And she has found it too,
Let's hope that each new race we meet,
Is brother – sister, too!

Ode to Denji

I may not know you very well,
But this I know is true,
You're following where your father leads,
And that's what you should do.

I know not where your future lies,
Or where your paths will lead,
I only know, that all you learn,
And every book you read,

Will help you, just as I have found,
Though sixty years ago,
I've tried to follow, all life through,
School mottos that I know.

'Aim High' my son, in all you do,
But still remember, too,
'Think on Higher Things', young man,
In everything you do.

Perfect Taste

As I sit here at my desk,
Wondering what to say,
I'm looking at a photograph,
That came here yesterday.

The picture is my granddaughter,
In graduation dress
The colour, such a lovely red,
The style, made to impress.

I placed it with my family groups,
But even so, it shone,
For all the beauty that was there,
It joins the growing throng.

She has a lot of studies yet,
Before her goal is met,
But she has set her sights up high,
And that she'll not forget.

And now, my dear, keep strong and true,
I hope you find your goal,
The road of life is long and hard,
Go for it! heart and soul!

Linette 1990

Ode to Helga

And now my little girl's all grown up,
The thought just makes me smile,
You've grown just like your Mother, dear,
You go the 'Extra Mile'.

More than once, she did just that,
Old friends, I don't forget,
We all came to this fair land,
I hope we don't regret.

We did it all for such as you,
We thought of our boys, too,
At forty years, we ventured forth,
To start our life anew.

They say at forty, life begins!
I hope it's true for you,
Let your life be one of love,
To those around you, too.

You've planned your future life, it seems,
Including someone who
Will care for you, your whole life through,
May God bless both of you!

Memories

Long years ago, 'twas fifty five,
We travelled north to find
A livelihood in this fair land,
With others of our kind.

We all had come with hopes held high,
From lands across the sea,
Our native lands, still troubled lands,
When will the world be free?

And so we made some lifelong friends,
We watched our children grow,
Her little girl, my little boy,
Together in the snow.

But in the year of fifty-eight,
We found our friendship true,
She took full charge of hers and mine,
While we kept vigil through

The long, long days and nights, we sat
Watching by his bed. So cold,
But Someone else was watching, too,
And ere the year was old,

My son was home, with years of pain,
Ahead of him, till now,
In ninety-two we meet again,
Renewed our friendly vow.

For she has had her troubles, too,
Her faith has kept her strong,
We both know the trials we face,
Our faith will keep us strong.

Her little girl, my little boy,
Are forty years old now,
Their dear ones with them all life long,
We thank God for our joy.

Bruni

Will You be Mine?

'Twas on a day in ninety-two,
In fact 'twas sweet July,
Did he go down on bended knee?
Oh, no, that's all gone by!

I wish for them, great happiness,
And may they learn to share,
Their dreams and plans together now,
May love be always there.

Steven and Karen

74

Music in your Life

The first time that I spoke to you,
I knew you were the one,
The one to bring him happiness,
When both of you are one.

There'll be such music everywhere,
Wherever you may be,
Your life will be a sonnet then,
For all your friends to see.

If music be the food of love,
Play on! and you will find,
True meaning in the life you live,
A blessing to mankind.

Thank you, Lord

'Thank you, Lord' each day I say,
When morning gilds the sky,
The sleep He gave, three hours or more,
While in my bed I lie.

For rest and stillness of the night,
In spite of endless pain,
Gives me the strength I seem to need,
In sunshine and in rain.

Each night I thank Him for the day,
He gave me to enjoy,
For there are many more like me,
Each moment is a joy.

True Christian Love

The last time that I went to church,
'Twas many months ago,
My son that took me was in pain,
But no one was to know.

How I sat that service through,
I never more shall know,
On leaving at the service close,
We shook hands at the door.

I'd had enough of watching pain,
Of one so brave and true,
And all I got, was a hand, so limp.
My tears meant nothing, too.

But one that took my son's two hands,
And held them with his two,
He looked into his eyes, and said,
'You're in great pain, aren't you?

Can my son and I forget?
Oh no, it's printed deep,
No matter how long we shall live,
Such love is there to keep.

Roland

All God's Children, Everywhere!

'Twas in the year of seventy-eight,
I met this little girl,
She and her Mother joined my son,
To make their life unfurl.

My son took her, just as his own,
And life was just a dream,
A baby boy soon joined them all,
And they made quite a team.

And as she grew, there were some times,
When life was true to form,
But years pass by, and troubles too,
She weathered every storm.

I know not where your future lies,
Or where your paths may lead,
I only know that all you learn,
And every book you read,

Will help you, just as I have found,
Though sixty years ago,
I've tried to follow, all life through,
School mottos that I know.

'Aim High', my girl, in all you do,
But still remember too,
'Think of Higher Things', my dear,
In everything you do.

Linette

My Life with God

Lord, I have so much to say,
Don't know where to begin,
There are so many in this world,
In pain, just like I'm in.

And yet, I must be thankful, Lord,
For giving me these years,
Though every day is quite a trial,
And brings my Mother's tears.

Now I find I cannot do,
Things I trained to live,
Thirty years You've helped me through,
Instead of only five.

'Twas only five in fifty-eight
But You had other plans,
And now I'm grateful for the chance,
I've had to do those plans.

But Lord, it is so hard to bear,
Accept the prospect now,
Of finding something else to do,
And still fulfil Your vow.

For I have learnt, my Mother's prayer,
Whatever state I'm in,
To be content, if Lord it is,
Your wish for me within.

Show me how to be of use,
To fill my future years,
Let me see the woods again,
The beavers and the bears.

For it is there, I get my strength,
Among the things you gave,
Oh! may we all preserve the things,
For future friends to save.

Roland

Young Love

There was a boy, there was a girl,
So many years ago,
'Twas fifty-nine to be exact,
This day! My! years do go!

We met at the garden gate,
Of the Manse, no less,
He knew the maid, so quiet and shy,
We were all pals, I guess.

And as we talked, of this and that,
He had a bag of sweets,
He handed them around to us,
A custom he repeats.

We went together, as we planned,
To the garden fair,
A Chapel gathering every year,
Held in the Autumn there.

We courted, two years and a half,
Until that day in May,
When we became as one for life,
In our Chapel, far away.

Where did all those years go to?
Our Chapel still is strong,
With all the births of children, five,
Recorded, and belong!

Autumn Joy

Oh, what a weekend I have had!
First I had my hair-do,
On coming home, my dear young ones,
From far away there, too.

They brought me flowers, to show they care,
And brought us lots of news,
We sat and chatted over lunch,
And stated all our views.

They brought me music, that I'd asked,
The best one they could find,
Music of another age,
The future of their kind.

It lifted me out of myself,
Into a world above,
I know that I shall often play
This music that they love.

Where would we be without such art?
For that was very clear,
With little shivers down the spine,
At other times, a tear.

They came to visit friends of theirs,
And do a job for Dad,
Before the winter storms begin,
Some they've already had.

Tomorrow they'll be gone away,
But there's always the phone,
There's Christmas, then holidays planned,
With my good friends, alone.

They all have had their troubles, too
But happy they will be,
Grateful that they've all been spared,
They'll bring their joys to me.

Goodbye to Della!

He went up to his favourite spot,
He goes there every fall,
When leaves are turning, red and gold,
And peace lies over all.

He goes there with one dream in mind,
To see once more his falls,
The Della Falls, the highest yet,
The beauty of it calls.

He sees the otter, beaver too,
And eagles flying high,
But as he went this time again,
He felt the time was nigh.

When, boating, climbing, walking, too
Are just too much to do,
And so he said a good-bye prayer,
To Della Falls, Adieu.

But wait! This need not be the end,
Strathcona's big and wide,
And much there is for him to do,
If just to be a Guide.

He carved himself a Scouter's Staff,
He knew the time had come,
When this would be his trusty guide,
He'll make it! Life's not done!!

Roland

Loved Ones Abroad

I have so many friends around,
But those I value most,
Are those who three score years and ten
And live from coast to coast.

But there are two who live alone,
Their dear son passed away,
But they still have a daughter dear,
Who lives so far away.

But as the year so swiftly moves,
Towards this Christmastide,
There will be joy, around the tree,
While she and son abide.

For she lives across the sea,
With dear one and their son,
Now she and grandson, soon will come,
To share in Christmas fun.

They won't be here for very long,
For they have much to do,
For he is entering High School now,
The way I used to go.

'Aim High' my son, my motto read,
But do remember, too,
'Think on Higher Things', dear boy,
In everything you do.

Christmas Wishes

Things have been so hard this year,
For Dad and Mum and me,
So now I hope this Christmastide,
Will bring what it should be.

A time for thinking what it means,
To live a life like ours,
Thankful for each day that breaks,
And all the daylight hours.

Accept my wishes with this card,
For fun, and laughter, too,
And may the year of ninety-three,
Bring happiness, to you.

Uncle Roland 1992

Lest We Forget

I sat and watched the service held
Around the cenotaph today,
I saw the flags of every nation
Represented for that day.

I saw the faces of the men
The medals proudly worn,
The women too with greying hair
Whose part was played each morn.

I joined and sang the anthems too
Along with all the rest.
'Land of Hope and Glory' – yes,
'Abide with Me' – then rest.

Rest for silence, at the time,
When all was still for thought,
Remembering those who've gone before,
When freedom had been bought.

Each poppy wreath was set in place
According to their rank,
It took me back a long long way,
There's only One to thank.

For I was born when war began
And as I grew the tales
My Mother told me of the war
Have stayed, all through my trails.

She told me of the airship huge,
On dark and weary night,
Caught in the searchlight in the sky
Just like a shuttle might.

She watched it there, went back and forth,
For there was no escape;
These and more were told to me
Until I saw myself.

The men marching to the camp,
Their final papers sought,
For they had done what had to be,
And freedom had been bought.

Another twenty years went by,
I had two baby boys,
And on those bright and moonlit nights
We waited with no joy.

We'd go into the garden fair,
And look up in the sky,
The planes were there – ours or theirs?
We sighed as they passed by.

But there were many many more
Who sought the way of peace,
I hope 'twas not in vain they died
For all the wars to cease.

For I have friends who know all this,
For they remember too,
But one who knows both sides of war,
For me is one so true.

The wrangling that goes on so much
It's very hard to stem,
Let them rest in peace, Dear Lord,
We will remember them.

11th November, 1992

Our Little Home

I often look around the town
At houses big and small,
Some of them have gabled roofs,
I like them most of all.

Some have carports, sundecks, pools,
A pond for goldfish too,
With bedrooms up and bedrooms down,
And floors all shiny new.

But one that I like most of all
Is small and neat and clean,
Just big enough for all our needs,
The best one I have seen.

A house is made of wood and stone,
And everything that's new;
But homes are built of family ties,
And living hearts so true.

Fifty Years Together

Another year has come and gone,
The Golden Ones are here,
But here you are together still,
Dreaming without fear.

You've made the journey, side by side,
The road was often rough,
You've had your ups and downs, I know,
Sometimes the work was tough.

But you were brought together, then,
By One who knows the best,
He knew your love would get you through
He knew you'd stand the test.

And now, my friends, we know not what
May lie in years ahead,
We only know your love is strong,
Just as the day you wed.

Revd. Harold and Norma Wingfield
50th Anniversary.

God Bless Them Both

Another lovely day for me,
My grandson and his love,
Have told me of their news today,
A union made above.

They both have studies yet to do,
To make their future sure,
But they will make their life as one,
When life is more secure.

May they be blessed from this day on,
So near to Christmas Day,
'Twas on great-grandpa's birthday, too,
Good Luck, and Bless this day.

Geoff and Jody engaged.

Happy Birthday, Weekly Friend

Happy Birthday, weekly friend!
I hope your day goes well,
You keep me company, every week,
With some little tale to tell.

I wish for you a lovely day,
Find cares and worries gone,
And may the light of this new dawn,
Make life a brand new song.

So Sean, and dear Deanna, too,
Make her day so bright,
For, someday, she'll be old, like me
You two, will make things right.

Sharon.

Jesus' Birthday

Happy Birthday, little one,
In the stable bare,
Mother Mary, kneeling there,
Showing love and care.

When each Christmas comes around,
And festive thoughts abound,
Let us stop and think awhile,
Just what the world has found.

There should be thoughts of peace and love,
For those in need of care,
And not the price of gifts we buy,
Instead of simple prayer.

May we all resolve to try,
To ease, just one of His,
Whole days are often dark and grey,
'Twas all He asks – just this!

Midnight Service, Christmas.
Bhagwan and Gail.

Friendly Care

I know a man, a kindly man,
He's like a son to me,
Although I have five of my own,
His nature's plain to see.

Four of mine are scattered far,
But one is always near,
His health has troubled him for years
But help was always near.

Some say, 'You'll get no help at all,
Until you quit your work'.
My son, a quitter, Oh no thanks,
His duty he'll not shirk!

For he has faith, that One above,
Together with his friend,
Will pull him through, in work and play,
Until the very end.

When Mother needs some special care,
Permission, my son sought,
'You go! Our Mothers mean much more
Than all that can be bought'.

These words mean much more to him,
Than all that money buys,
Such care is printed deep inside,
They'll greet each day's sunrise!

Mike

Believers All

I wrote a letter from the heart,
My soul was troubled, sore,
My little world was upside down,
I couldn't take much more.

All the years that I'd been taught.
For seventy-eight or more,
All the truths, my Father spoke,
Did from his pulpit pour.

My Mother followed his advice,
And led me on that way,
But times have changed, not for the best,
And I must change, and pray.

And then one day two friends called in,
They came from foreign shores,
Their faith unknown to me was true,
And taught me to explore.

The man, not of my colour, read,
Then bent his head and said,
'Oh! there is such hurt in there
Why make your tears be shed?'

'For all your life and family, too,
Have followed in His way,
Hold on! to what your Father said,
Your faith will always stay'.

Bhagwan

My Daughters

My life has been a fantasy,
With sons that number five,
'Look at all the daughters you
Will have by seventy-five!'

I now have four daughters fine,
They all have work to do,
With such a change in life today,
Their lives are full, that's true.

But I have found, for many years,
Together with these four,
Two other girls, so kind and true,
'Daughters', to the core.

They help me always look my best,
In sunshine and in rain,
I know they're there, if I should need,
Their help in times of strain.

My life has been a fantasy,
With all that life can give,
But through it all, I feel that these
Dear 'Daughters', help me live.

Ode to Wesley

And now my grandson's growing up,
His birthday time is here;
He's quite a little man by now,
Don't grow too fast, my dear.

You are my youngest little boy,
So soon you'll all be grown.
I hope as years go by for you,
Your hopes and dreams you'll own.

So here's to you – my Birthday Boy,
Have a happy day!
But while you grow into a man
Remember Mum – in May.

Save a Place for me, Dear!

When our friends have gone ahead,
We feel the loss so deep,
But we must not be in despair,
For they are but asleep.

I have known her many years,
In fact 'twas sixty-nine,
There were but nine of us that day,
All with one design.

Those concerned with temperate things,
We wear our little bow,
'For God and Home and every Land'
For purity to show.

She was our leader from that day,
She guided us along;
Her mind was full of teaching truth,
She helped us all grow strong.

She worked in all the ways she could,
To spread the Christian views,
She taught the youth, the way to face,
Their future life anew.

Sure there'll be an empty chair,
We will all miss her so,
Her work was done, God took her home,
We'll meet again, we know!

Betty

Thank You, one and all

I've just been laid on bed of pain,
In fact, in two-o-two,
And as I lay I watched the care,
As work they had to do.

The one that came to me at first,
She spoke her name so clear,
She tended to me every day,
Her nursing skill was clear.

The one in blue, was helpful, too,
She changed my bandaged hand,
She left some part of it for now,
She did each job at hand.

The one in pink, so quick and slim,
She rushed from place to place,
And yet her limbs are needing care,
But still she'll come through grace.

The one in white, with smiling eyes,
Her fair hair taken while
She wears a barrett at the neck,
A very pleasant style.

And oh! there were so many more,
The coloured with the white,
They all were trained to do their job,
So cheerful and so bright.

There was a man, that pleased me most,
But oh the kindness shown,
His training was no doubt, the best,
His colour, not my own.

My Doctors too, I'll not forget,
Their knowledge proved so true,
We all have cause for 'Thanks', to them,
Especially two-o-two!

February 1993

Ode to a New Grandson

How do I feel, this day of days?
I've waited for so long,
And now I have a new young man,
Our family to belong.

My dear granddaughter, long has known,
That he would be the one,
The one to make her life complete,
And share the rain and sun.

I seldom see them, life is full,
For they are miles away,
I know he'll care, as none before,
To guide towards that day.

For they both know, the good and true,
Each day is theirs alone,
But they will spend each moment wise,
Until their task is done.

Marc and Lorelei.

What Does it Mean?

What does it mean when two in love,
Declare their future vow?
Do they always have to wear
Proverbial rings, just now?

Oh no, I think not, love is strong,
And future plans are made,
Those 'little hands' that once I saw,
When in her cot she laid.

'What will they do? Where will they go?'
My thoughts for her were said,
'Will her finger wear a ring?'
Oh yes, when they are wed.

There is so much that they must do,
Before that day next year,
My son, his daughter, and his son!
I hope we'll both be there.

Lorelei and Marc.

Grandma's Thoughts

I wrote among my memoirs old,
Many years ago,
In fact it was in seventy-three,
October, it was so.

A baby boy was born that night,
We knew all was not well,
A journey many miles was made,
For doctor's help to tell.

And as he grew, 'twas plain to see,
That problems he would need,
Something that was very wrong,
With organs used to feed.

But as he grew, as young boys will,
His nature he revealed,
Always there to lend a hand,
In work of any field.

But Grandmas are supposed to sit,
And watch the world go by,
Our views, and teachings, no one needs,
We watch, and wonder why.

Someday, we may be needed, too,
As things, just now, are wrong,
But we will just await the call,
That we still do belong.

Look to the Future

As the years go rolling by,
Two thousand, soon 'twill be,
We, the Grandmas, watch and wait,
What will the outcome be?

The children now have gone their way,
Each with their chosen life,
And now we watch the young ones choose
Careers for their life.

Some seem to follow paths of law,
With discipline severe,
Others like their minds to work,
With computers near.

And some prefer the great outdoors,
With all things great and small,
All things bright and beautiful,
They know who made them all.

I hope they choose the path that's right,
The one thing they can do,
To show their fellowman the way,
The honest, and the true.

Let us be Thankful

When our homeland's far away,
And years have passed between,
Since last our feet were on that soil,
And all that that may mean,

You think of years that you were there,
For forty years or more,
And forty more have almost gone,
Sometimes our hearts are sore.

So many changes have been made,
Across the waters wide,
We hear, we listen and we read,
The 'progress' on each side.

And now we look around us here,
At beauty we can see,
We have our memories of our home,
As always they shall be.

So now we watch the world go by,
There's trouble everywhere,
But we are thankful to be here,
For all of us to share.

Advancing Years

'What is this world so full of care,
If we've not time to stand and stare',
These words we've known since childhood days,
But they meant nothing in those days.

When we're young, the days are long,
Full of ways to make us strong,
Not a moment we must waste,
Time is precious, let's make haste!

Round and round the world we go,
Learning all there is to know,
Way up high! down far below!
Which way will our future go?

Some of us will live and learn,
And others for a living earn,
By gifts and talents, they can use,
For making troubled times reduce.

But those of us, beyond this time,
We stand and stare – we've got the time
At all the beauty, made to see,
For truth, strength and faith from THEE.

Make Time to Listen

When you're feeling all alone,
The place is also strange,
Nothing seems to go quite right,
You wish that it would change.

There comes a man, with knowledge true,
He sees your trouble, understands,
And listens, while the story's told,
He has a soothing hand.

Your mind and heart are just too full,
You cannot hold it back,
He stands beside, as tears they flow,
And waits, while peace is back.

Then speaks with understanding heart,
With all he has to say,
No haste to hurry on his way,
On such a busy day.

His manner, quiet and caring too,
I never shall forget,
I thank God for him every day,
His memory lingers yet.

February 1993

Science? – or a Miracle?

I was in the hospital,
A little while ago,
This was nothing new to me,
Folks dashing to and fro.

But as I sat upon my bed,
Waiting for the call,
To be prepared, as usual,
For trip along the hall.

I wore a dressing-gown, my own,
It was a pretty blue,
My own pyjamas, dusty pink,
All would be changed, I knew.

I sat and waited, half an hour,
Before my theatre time,
But no one came, to do the jobs,
That must be done in time.

The very next thing I recall,
Was in my comfy bed,
On my right side, as they knew,
'Twas what had all been said.

I opened up my sleepy eyes,
And saw someone sincere,
She spoke so softly, full of care,
'It's over now, my dear'.

My right hand bandaged expertly,
My feet, too, 'slightly bent!'
As in the film, 'The King and I',
'Life was a Puzzlement'.

With backs like mine, nerves all trapped,
My right side is the best,
With pillow at my back, they know,
They all knew, like the rest.

How I got from – 'there to here'!
Perhaps I shouldn't care,
Was it – science of this age?
A Miracle – or Prayer?

February 1993

Give Him the Best!

I have some friends that live quite close,
They're very dear to me,
They have a daughter, miles away,
With dear one, son makes three.

They get their news, through mail and phone,
It keeps them all so near,
And now, the young one, in his teens,
His future path is clear.

For Mum and Dad, and Grand-ones, too,
All chose for him the best,
Oh how I wish that all of mine,
Had grown to pass the test!

But they just have the only one,
And want for him the best,
The discipline and teaching he will get,
He'll get through every test.

If I had never left my home,
My boys all would have been,
So proud of training value there,
But all turned out serene.

Old Friends

I had a friend call in today,
We hadn't met in years,
We talked of things, the good, the bad,
The laughter, and the tears.

'Twas nice to chat of times gone by,
I told him all my news,
And so we sat, with cup in hand,
Exchanging each our views.

He lives alone, since Father died,
Sometimes the day seems long,
He has his friends, who hunt and fish,
He often goes along.

New friends are needed all the time,
But Oh! what a joy to see,
And old, old friend from out the past,
Call in and chat with me.

Look to the East

There is a group of friends I know,
They meet for friendship true,
The flowers with lighted candles form,
Artistry shown anew.

We care for sick and ageing ones,
And some are lonely, too,
And yet there are those in this world,
Who doubt the good we do.

When in the centre, form a cross,
A symbol of our life?
Our brothers and our sisters, too,
To follow through their life?

We train the young ones to become,
Like all our virtues true,
Oh may they follow t'wards the East,
Just as we try to do.

Mother's Day

Long ago and far away,
The day was held in March,
'Mothering Sunday', was its name,
With clothes all fresh with starch.

My Father gave to Mother dear,
The first that he could find,
Of English violets, so rare,
The finest of its kind.

But many years have passed since then,
And Mother's Day is here,
We Mothers, who are Grandmas now,
We watch, and wonder here.

Will the Great-Grands, gather round,
When special days are here?
Will they treasure memories like,
My Mothers violets, so dear?

'You'll Always have me'

It was the first phone call today,
It came from far away,
My dearest little granddaughter,
It really made my day.

She told me all her news, to date,
Their work they do each day,
And all improvements to their home,
For it's all theirs, to pay.

There is the bathroom, perfect peach,
A shade I love to see,
With all the fittings, all to match,
How lovely it will be!

The kitchen they have yet to do,
But that I know will be,
Just like the rest, in perfect taste,
For this their home, we'll see.

We spoke of family, as we live,
Apart, and understand
The little aspects, true to life,
We face them hand-in-hand.

And so this is my Mother's Day,
My family I shall see,
At least, my dearest faithful few,
She said, 'You'll always have me'!

116

'One, Two, Button my shoe'

'One, two, button my shoe,
Three, four, knock at my door',
These were the verses I recall,
Long ago, when I was small.

I wonder what they hear today?
Grandma, knows just what to say,
As she looks after, one, two, three,
And Mother struggles to be free.

Free of stresses, yet unknown,
Holding her from doing her own,
Things a mother loves to do,
For little ones, just one or two.

She lies ensnared in nerves that seem
At twenty-two to end her dream,
But encouragement and hope,
Along with aids, will help her cope.

May we hope and pray that soon,
Those who can travel to the moon,
Will find among their expertise,
Some help from science, for such as these.

'What is in Your Hand?'

As we read of days gone by,
On pages specially fine,
Of parables, that make you think.
About your life and mine.

Things that you were trained to do,
For men, and women, too,
There comes a time, some young, some old,
To think of talents, new.

'What is in your hand, today?'
Our Maker wants to know,
'Talents that I gave to you
Now show the way to go.'

'Use them well, in every way,
I knew someday you would
Skills you never knew you had
Will now show that you could.'

'What is in your hand today?'
The tools of life are there,
Pass your knowledge on to those,
To use, and those who care.

You will reap the benefit,
By watching how they use
The 'Talents in your hand today'
For future years to use.

Enough, and to spare!

'My old man', from 'over there',
Loves his garden fair,
He prunes and sprays, and hoes and mows,
But, this year, just one pear.

Yes! there was just one, this year,
But, Oh dear, plums to spare,
There were so many, friends could have,
But he must have his share.

So, there we were, with bottles, twelve,
And pans and syrup, too,
But, Oh goodness, what a mess!
When over boiled the brew!

Anyway, the stove, the floor,
All had an extra clean,
And now he has his year's supply,
All where they can be seen!

Follow the Leader

There was a game we used to play,
When we were young and free;
As we children gathered round,
And chased around each tree.

We ran around the great outdoors,
Life was good just then,
We had no worries, cares, just fun,
When all of us were ten.

But life is not all fun and games,
As we found as we grew,
Each of us went separate ways,
Away to pastures new.

One always chose the 'great outdoors',
His work and hobbies, too,
When he had a day to spare,
He sought the lakes so blue.

His favourite spot, in his canoe,
Was twenty miles or more,
Along the waters, sometimes rough,
To trails, beyond the shore.

One day, when rowing slowly home,
For he was kept alive
By faith, and prayer and will power, too,
For twenty years and five.

He'd spent his life in keeping fit,
And as he rowed this day,
He'd noticed as he left the shore,
A group around the bay.

Young men, who, training in this skill,
With leaders, teaching, too,
And now he wondered, how they fared,
'Twas quite a length to do.

When he arrived upon the shore,
There were two missing crew,
So, although tired, and getting dark,
He went, the way he knew.

He found them both, in their canoe,
Slumped o'er their oars just 'beat',
Lost and hungry, all alone,
What's this? A friend to greet.

For years, a Search and Rescue, man,
He knew, just what to do,
Two chocolate bars, his thermos, too,
A word, 'Hello, you two.'

They travelled slowly, miles it seemed,
Talking all the time,
'Follow me, I'll get you there,
Try to keep in line.'

His childhood memory, served him well,
He stayed ahead, two feet.
Encouraged them to follow him,
His plan proved quite a feat.

Was he on the lake, that day,
For reasons, we don't know?
Were there lessons to be learnt
By those there, as they grow?

Roland

Be Prepared

He went up to his usual haunt,
The Della Falls, and Trail,
He set his camp, and made the climb,
The light began to fail.

There were others at the camp,
And all were quite upset,
For one, who thought he knew it all,
Had still not come back yet.

They looked across, towards the climb,
And saw his jacket there,
He'd hung it on a branch up there,
He didn't seem to care.

This life long scout knew what to do,
He said, 'I'll get him down.'
He had equipment he would need,
No need to fret or frown.

To, 'Be Prepared' was something he had
Always learnt to do,
So off he went, with torches, ropes,
For jobs he'd have to do.

For Hypothermia, on his mind,
As always it has been,
For twenty-five's a long, long, time,
And much of it he's seen.

He crossed the growth of evergreens,
And climbed to where he saw,
The jacket hanging on a tree,
And took it, with much more.

He reached the man, who held on tight,
'Frozen' is the term,
When scared to leave your safety hold,
Although your help was firm.

He pulled him off, by talking firm,
And yet he let him know,
That faith, and trust, in those who help,
Will show the way to go.

So, roped together, jackets warm,
They slowly made it down,
Across the patch of undergrowth,
To where they could lie down.

Oh the joy when they all met!
And supper was prepared,
An invitation, and their thanks,
The 'Scouter', knew they cared.

Roland

Two of a Kind

There once was a seed that was planted by love,
And nurtured with love and with care,
But God liked the look of this little seed,
And said, 'I'll make it a pair!'

So, these two little girls, they grew, and grew,
With hair, fair as newly spun gold,
They live still quite near, but not quite as close,
As God made them, one day old!

Carol and Karen.

Father's Day

To love someone all through the year,
And know he loves you too,
On Father's day, to let him know,
Gives happiness he knew.'

'He's known to me. deep down inside,
I never can repay,
All the forces in my life,
He's guided all the way.'

These are thoughts, my sons express,
Those from far and near,
I think he knew them, in his heart,
All through his troubled year.

And now today, a lovely day,
One took him out to see,
A look at all the old, old cars,
And things that used to be.

He'll go back in time, today,
His sons, and grandson, too
While one of them, restores these things,
His memory goes back, too.

A Brighter Day is Coming

These words shine, as no sun shone,
Upon a greeting card,
My son, who understands my pain,
Had brought it on a card.

For I have been, a week or more,
And all my doctors too,
So puzzled by the helpless pain,
That came for two weeks through.

But when I woke again today,
My leg, I found, would move,
Just a teeny-weeny bit,
But there was hope to prove.

And so he brought me this sweet card,
'To hope today was good
And tomorrow better still',
His faith does what it should.

It gives me hope, a will to live,
And do the best I can,
Both he and I know what it means,
To live, with God's own plan.

Roland

Gooseberry Pie

That man of mine, from Lancashire,
Is far away from home like me,
Although my home was t'other side
Beside the river Tee.

He's in the garden, at the moment,
Picking from the tree,
Gooseberries, though very small,
They'll make a pie for tea.

When first we came to this fair land,
So many things we sought,
Tasty morsels we enjoyed,
We found could not be bought.

For many years, both up and down,
This island home of ours,
But could we find a gooseberry?
We searched for many hours.

And so, at last, we bought a bush,
In fact, I think 'twas two,
And now we have a row of them,
Enough for friends so true.

Friends like us, who tried to find,
Things we used to eat,
And also new friends, we had made,
Who'd never tried this treat.

And so it is with many things,
When new lands you may find,
You search until you find the things,
That seem to ease your mind.

It makes you feel you're more at home,
Enjoying what you've found,
And all because, a dear old man,
Grows gooseberries, by the pound!

Thanks! – to you Both

We went away, a while ago,
When pain was not too strong,
A few days in a warmer clime,
My son planned all along.

He did the very best he could,
His wife, with details, too,
They showed us sights, all new to us,
We ne'er would think were true.

On coming home, a greeting card,
And flowers, waiting there,
A card, that read, 'Just thanks to you
For all the help you share!'

For this son knows the meaning of
The pain we both are in,
But when you understand the toil,
It helps to know, we'll win!

My 'Special' One

My great-grandchild will soon be here,
For all the world to see,
Maybe Jordan by the sea,
Or maybe Linden Lee.

It matters not the names they choose,
As long as all is well,
A little boy, a little girl,
Only time will tell.

I know his name is Justin,
Or Jordan, it might be,
But in my heart, my little boy,
Will be my Linden Lee.

Or maybe Jordan by the sea,
It matters not to me,
The first one I have ever seen.
Of six that came from me.

These were names they chose for me,
To help me to recall,
Little places far away,
When I was three feet tall!

Other names this little one,
Will have of family fame,
But I shall always think of my
Child with English name.

This one is the only one,
To have a name from 'home',
A name I shall remember as
These names brings thoughts of home.

Jordan

Teenage Morals

I know that times have changed a lot,
Since I was just a girl,
But this one thing I truly know,
Her talents will unfurl.

She was a girl, who many years,
She cared for those in pain,
She noticed one, who though she loved,
In sunshine and in rain.

Was not prepared to follow her,
And leave his wrongful ways,
And so, she chose the good and true,
With parents, and their ways.

She'd made her plans, to care for those,
Whose life is grim with pain,
Her Father, too, has given his life,
To those whose life is strain.

She's not alone, she has her dream,
And parents' full support,
She has her friends, and some true kin,
And those her studies, taught.

She passed her grades, and got her scroll,
And now she's lots to do,
For I am close, two sons close too,
We all will help her through.

Silken Flowers

As on my velvet couch I lie,
Several times a day,
To rest my poor old leg and back,
It is the only way.

But as I lie, I look around,
At treasures on the wall,
The first I see is straight ahead,
Hanging up so tall.

It is a basket, coloured pink,
It's filled with flowers she made,
A mixture all arranged by one
Who did it without aid.

She made it just for me to see,
She knew I had to stay,
In my little house all day,
And look at her bouquet.

The flowers, they are made of silk,
She knew they would not fade,
I had no need to tend or water,
Just look at what she made.

She hung it there at Christmastime,
In fact 'twas ninety-two,
And when 'twas time to take them down,
The cards, and trimmings too,

She asked if I would leave it there,
And there it will remain,
For now I see the silken flowers,
And quietly say her name.

Jody

Our Little Corner

There's been so many changes made,
On the corner by my home,
A long way off, in sixty-three,
'Twas just a peaceful zone.

With little houses on both sides,
And trees for fruit and flowers,
The mail box just across the road,
We waited for the hour.

Always bringing news from home,
And local bills to pay.
Life was slow, and traffic, too,
With carts with loads of hay.

And then one day, in seventy-four,
I wrote, 'Death of a tree',
For men were there with saws and things,
To change the view for me.

The little house with red tin roof,
And cherry trees and all,
Everything was cleared away,
For concrete building tall.

And then the next door on that side,
With hobby farm as well,
All went the way of progress, too,
A building, painted well.

And now the houses, close to us,
Are changing faces, too,
Some for businesses have gone,
Others stay, the old folks too.

Then last year, the piece of land,
Was sold, 'twas ninety-two,
And old, old houses on the lot,
Fell to the builders, too.

There was a stand of lovely trees,
But now they are all gone,
And now I look to highway wide,
And see what's going on.

And then today, this lot next door,
Across the avenue,
Men with sextants, and their tools,
Preparing something new.

But all this time, for thirty years,
We've kept our garden fair,
With roses, well known all around,
My hubby's special care.

My 'Wooden Leg'

I've just come back from hospital,
A few miles north of here,
I went to have a strong support,
So safety will be near.

For I have worn a lighter one,
For near a month 'tis now,
Because the doctors seem to think,
Something's wrong somehow.

I should be grateful for their help,
But Oh! it's not like me,
To be restricted in this state,
What has to be, will be!

My leg has caused me trouble now,
For months, and years, it seems,
But now it's tired of struggling on,
Without some other means,

To help, and so I find that I,
Must use the talents, now,
That I was given by the One
Who knew, what I know now!

One of the Best

He lived for over half his life,
With drama and the arts,
And then one day his health began,
To cause concern, in parts.

He sort the best advice he could,
But answers were not new,
In these strange times in which we live,
His trouble was not new.

There were new things that he could try,
But nothing seemed to do,
There are so many, just like him,
Men and women too.

Even scientific men,
Are doing what they can,
In trying to find relief for these,
Stricken like this man.

But he will not 'call it a day',
Until his work is done,
For he has much he wants to do,
In teaching, work and fun.

Someday, someone will be found,
With knowledge his views, shares,
But until then, we'll hope and pray,
That 'Someone Upstairs' cares.

His future is as yet unknown,
Is filled with plans sublime,
So, as my son was told, in years gone by,
'It just was not his time'.

Bill Bixby

Heartaches

As I lie here to rest a while,
To help me through the day,
How times have changed, since we left home,
But here we all will stay.

There used to be an hour to spend,
With someone who would call,
Or maybe go out for a drive,
To see some favourite hall.

But we cannot move around,
And people's lives are full.
There is no time to stop and chat,
And home thoughts often pull.

To sit beside a cosy fire,
And watch the dancing flames,
To lean against the garden gate,
And know your neighbour's name,

Each of them you knew by name,
A Harry, Tom or Joe,
But now their names you can't pronounce,
So you just say 'Hello'.

There is a time for everything,
A time to come and go,
But Oh! to see again the streams,
So clear, so quiet and slow.

The old stone walls, around the fields,
With sheep a-grazing there,
I know there's progress everywhere,
But still there's land to spare.

Hills and dales, and crofters' homes,
Built to feel no dread,
How I envy those who dwell!
Where I was born and bred!

Bless this sixty-fifth day!

Sixty-five! Oh! deary me!
A long, long, way they've come,
But these dear people, we have known,
For twenty-five, and some.

They've made the trek, not always bright,
There were some grey times, too,
But life is meant to be just that!
Some dark days and some blue.

They're loved by all, both far and wide,
In many walks of life,
They've earned respect, and honour, too,
This man, and his dear wife.

And so we gather here, today,
To wish them all the best,
The best of what? There's only One
Who knows how much they're blest!

Claude and Edna

He Closed the 'Gap'

His family came from Lancashire,
And he was born there too,
His father was the best man when
Our vows were made so true.

His parents now have passed away,
And though he's over there,
Nine thousand miles across the sea,
He's never ceased to care.

There's ne'er a week goes by, or maybe
Two weeks it will be,
We hear him on the telephone,
To ask, how we might be.

He knows that all's not well, just now,
And mail today is slow,
So he makes sure, that all he hears,
Improvement, soon will show.

Over half his life has gone,
He's used it, well and true,
Knowledge that he's gained throughout,
Is proving useful, too.

For progress in this world today
In scientific ways,
He's finding that the proven facts,
He knows will pave the ways.

For now he is involved in things,
On both sides of the sea,
But still he ne'er forgets to phone,
And check the family.

Donald

Oh Happy Day!

They used to say, that sunny June,
Was chosen by the bride,
But this one chose July to be,
Her day-of-days, to bide.

Beside her groom, so tall, and straight,
Our grandson, one of seven,
May they be blessed from this day on,
A blessing sent from Heaven!

Steven and Karen

Her Island Haven

There is an island off our shores,
Just one of many there,
They're dotted up and down the straits,
You only go by air.

It is a very peaceful place,
Where one can stay and rest,
With just one general store for all,
With goods for every guest.

She went to stay, with Mum and Dad,
And little sister, too,
Grandma, Granddad, lived there too,
'Till Golden Years were through.

Time to think of what's to be,
And plan her future too,
In Grandma's house, quite near the beach,
She'll find a shell, or two.

I hope she brings home one for me,
So I have been there too,
I have some treasured ones at home,
From other places, too.

For like a jewel, just for her,
Set in a silver sea,
A time she needed, parents, too.
Reflect on things to be.

You'll go again, dear, some fine day,
But you'll not be alone,
There'll be the special one, that day,
Your Dad, and all his own.

Hold to your faith, dear, hope and strength,
There'll come a day, my love,
When you will show your Mum and Dad,
A gift, sent from above.

He'll have something that every man,
Just loves to call his own,
A Jordan, or a Linden Lee,
Don't keep it all alone!

Please come round sometime, to call,
I want to see you all!
For seventy-eight of years I've spent,
Without a Dad, so tall.

But you'll be there to take the place,
That my Mum had to fill,
Take care of her, you trained her right,
Her needs you will fulfil.

I'm lying here, there's no one home,
And looking at my flowers,
My silken flowers hanging there,
And counting out the hours.

Savary Island B.C.

My Dad's Legacy

My home's been filled with music for
As long as I have known,
For Father dear the organ played,
In home and chapel tone.

But when one year he passed away,
Left Mum, with daughters two,
The elder one, she studied hard,
And helped Mum as she grew.

She passed her grades, diplomas, too,
In keyboards, choral, too,
She played for silent films in town,
And dramas that were new.

But years went by, the war was here,
Her and her loved one sent,
Away to India, things to build,
For supervision, spent.

But still she had her piano, there,
The servants loved to hear,
But I came here, while she was there,
Our thoughts were kept sincere.

While still so young, I passed my tests,
And I too followed Dad,
With organ, choirs, piano, too,
For shore, to shore, I'm glad.

But now I've all that I could want,
With tunes on many tapes,
Captured, in this age and past,
That never will escape.

And so my Willis went its way,
To one I know will care,
As I have done for seventy years,
For music she can share.

She will remember, as I do.
Her Dad, and all he meant,
To her, and all around her, too,
I hope, she'll not repent.

David Calvert J.P.